ALL ABOUT INSECTS

ALL ABOUT LADYBUGS

by Karen Latchana Kenney

pogo

Ideas for Parents and Teachers

Pogo Books let children practice reading informational text while introducing them to nonfiction features such as headings, labels, sidebars, maps, and diagrams, as well as a table of contents, glossary, and index.

Carefully leveled text with a strong photo match offers early fluent readers the support they need to succeed.

Before Reading

- "Walk" through the book and point out the various nonfiction features. Ask the student what purpose each feature serves.
- Look at the glossary together. Read and discuss the words.

Read the Book

- Have the child read the book independently.
- Invite him or her to list questions that arise from reading.

After Reading

- Discuss the child's questions. Talk about how he or she might find answers to those questions.
- Prompt the child to think more. Ask: Ladybugs hibernate in winter. Why do they do this? Can you name other insects or animals that hibernate?

Pogo Books are published by Jump!
5357 Penn Avenue South
Minneapolis, MN 55419
www.jumplibrary.com

Copyright © 2024 Jump! International copyright reserved in all countries. No part of this book may be reproduced in any form without written permission from the publisher.

Library of Congress Cataloging-in-Publication Data

Names: Kenney, Karen Latchana author.
Title: All about ladybugs / by Karen Latchana Kenney.
Description: Minneapolis, MN: Jump!, Inc., [2024]
Series: All about insects | Includes index.
Audience: Ages 7-10
Identifiers: LCCN 2022052797 (print)
LCCN 2022052798 (ebook)
ISBN 9798885244367 (hardcover)
ISBN 9798885244374 (paperback)
ISBN 9798885244381 (ebook)
Subjects: LCSH: Ladybugs—Juvenile literature.
Classification: LCC QL596.C65 K468 2024 (print)
LCC QL596.C65 (ebook)
DDC 595.76/9—dc23/eng/20221110
LC record available at https://lccn.loc.gov/2022052797
LC ebook record available at https://lccn.loc.gov/2022052798

Editor: Jenna Gleisner
Designer: Emma Almgren-Bersie

Photo Credits: julichka/iStock, cover; macroworld/iStock, 1; Alex Staroseltsev/Shutterstock, 3; irin-k/Shutterstock, 4; Libor Vrska/Alamy, 5; thatmacroguy/Shutterstock, 6-7 (top); Manuel Balesteri/Alamy, 6-7 (bottom); Protasov AN/Shutterstock, 8-9 (ladybug); idizimage/iStock, 8-9 (background); Boxyray/Shutterstock, 10, 12-13 (top right); ViniSouza128/iStock, 11; Andia/Alamy, 12-13 (top left); Somyot Mali-ngam/Shutterstock, 12-13 (bottom); Nataba/iStock, 14; Andrew Darrington/Alamy, 15; Rolf Nussbaumer Photography/Alamy, 16-17; bo1982/iStock, 18-19; Wirestock/iStock, 20-21; alainolympus/iStock, 23.

Printed in the United States of America at Corporate Graphics in North Mankato, Minnesota.

TABLE OF CONTENTS

CHAPTER 1
Hey, Little Ladybug!......................4

CHAPTER 2
Life Cycle...................................10

CHAPTER 3
Staying Safe and Saving Plants..............14

ACTIVITIES & TOOLS
Try This!....................................22
Glossary.....................................23
Index..24
To Learn More................................24

CHAPTER 1

HEY, LITTLE LADYBUG!

A small red **insect** with black spots crawls on a blade of grass.

antennas

Its **antennas** smell and feel. A hard, round shell covers its body. What is this insect? It is a ladybug!

Ladybugs are beetles. More than 5,000 kinds of ladybugs live around the world. In some areas, they are called ladybirds.

Not all ladybugs are red and black. They can be many colors. The 16-spot ladybird is beige with black spots. The steel blue ladybird is shiny and dark blue.

DID YOU KNOW?

Why do some ladybugs have bright colors? The colors warn **predators** that the ladybug is **poisonous** if they eat it.

CHAPTER 1

16-spot ladybirds

steel blue ladybird

A ladybug lifts its hard **elytra**. Thin wings are folded underneath. They pop out quickly. Then, the ladybug takes off flying.

CHAPTER 1

TAKE A LOOK!

What are the parts of a ladybug? Take a look!

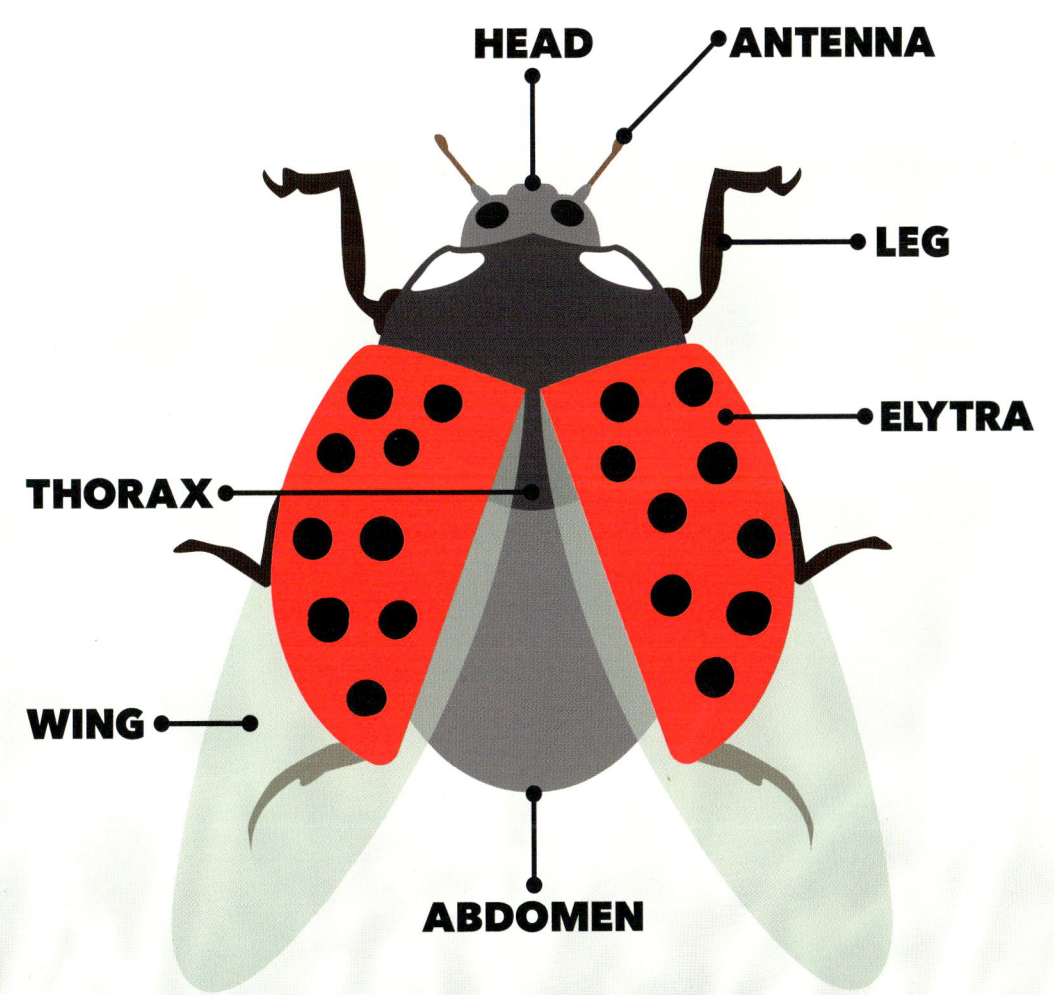

CHAPTER 1   9

CHAPTER 2
LIFE CYCLE

Female ladybugs lay tiny oval eggs on the undersides of leaves.

egg

larva

In a few days, **larvae** hatch from the eggs.

CHAPTER 2

molting larva

pupa

adult

Each larva **molts** around four times. Its skin splits, and the ladybug crawls out. It grows bigger each time it molts.

Next, the larva attaches to a leaf. Its skin hardens. Inside, it changes. This is the **pupa**. Soon, an adult comes out.

CHAPTER 3
STAYING SAFE AND SAVING PLANTS

Birds hunt adult ladybugs and larvae. Frogs, wasps, spiders, and flies also eat ladybugs.

Ladybugs protect themselves. Sometimes they play dead to trick predators. They release a kind of blood from their legs. It tastes and smells bad.

blood

CHAPTER 3 15

Ladybugs are not just **prey**. They are also fierce predators. They eat small insects called aphids. A ladybug can eat 5,000 aphids in its lifetime!

CHAPTER 3   17

Aphids harm plants. So do other insects that ladybugs eat, such as mealybugs and mites. These insects suck juices from stems, leaves, and roots. This kills the plants.

Some farmers release ladybugs to help their **crops**. The ladybugs quickly eat the plant-killing bugs.

DID YOU KNOW?

Ladybugs sometimes eat their own eggs! Why? They do this when they cannot find enough other food to eat.

Ladybugs also keep garden plants healthy and alive. Have you seen ladybugs crawling in a garden? They are nature's plant savers!

DID YOU KNOW?

In winter, ladybugs **hibernate**. Hundreds of them gather. They go under logs or inside homes. Why? It helps them stay warm.

CHAPTER 3

ACTIVITIES & TOOLS

TRY THIS!

WING COVERS

Ladybugs have hard elytra that cover their thin wings. Make a model of them with this activity!

What You Need:
- 2 paper plates
- black and red markers
- scissors
- 1 metal paper fastener
- black construction paper
- googly eyes (self-sticking)

❶ Take one paper plate. Color the side you eat on black.

❷ Take the other paper plate. Color the side you do not eat on red.

❸ Cut the red paper plate down the middle. Color black spots on each half.

❹ Cut a half-circle from the black construction paper. This will be the ladybug's head.

❺ Now put the pieces together. Put the black plate on the bottom. Lay the two red paper plate halves on top. Make one top corner go over the other.

❻ Push the metal paper fastener through the plates.

❼ Add the head under the plates. Push the metal paper fastener through. Open the ends to hold everything in place.

❽ Stick the googly eyes on the head.

❾ Now move the elytra. Can you see the black body beneath?

GLOSSARY

antennas: Feelers on the head of an insect.

crops: Plants grown as food.

elytra: The two wing cases of a ladybug or other kind of beetle.

hibernate: To spend the winter in a deep sleep to save energy and survive cold temperatures.

insect: A small animal with three pairs of legs, one or two pairs of wings, and three main body parts.

larvae: Insects in the stage of growth between eggs and pupae.

molts: Sheds an old, outer skin so that a new one can grow.

poisonous: Having a substance that can harm or kill an animal.

predators: Animals that hunt other animals for food.

prey: Animals that are hunted by other animals for food.

pupa: An insect in the stage of growth between larva and adult.

ACTIVITIES & TOOLS

INDEX

antennas 5, 9
aphids 17, 18
blood 15
colors 6
crops 18
eggs 10, 11, 18
elytra 8, 9
flying 8
hibernate 21
larvae 11, 13, 14

mealybugs 18
mites 18
molts 13
plants 18, 21
poisonous 6
predators 6, 15, 17
prey 17
pupa 13
spots 4, 6
wings 8, 9

TO LEARN MORE

Finding more information is as easy as 1, 2, 3.

❶ **Go to www.factsurfer.com**

❷ **Enter "ladybugs" into the search box.**

❸ **Choose your book to see a list of websites.**

24 ACTIVITIES & TOOLS